The soldiers in Harry's section of the veterinary corps liked having Winnie as their mascot. Harry is sitting in the middle row, second from the left. [*Archives of Manitoba, Colebourn, Harry (N10477)*]

Soldiers loved having their picture taken with Winnie.
[*Archives of Manitoba, Colebourn, Harry (N10470)*]

Winnie quickly became used to the many horses in the military camp. [*Archives of Manitoba, Colebourn, Harry (N10471)*]

Winnie was an expert tree climber.
[*Archives of Manitoba, Colebourn, Harry (N10468)*]

For Donovan and his animals—
May all your adventures be magnificent.
—S. M. W.

For Malachi and Lily
—J. D. V.

Henry Holt and Company, LLC / *Publishers since 1866*
175 Fifth Avenue, New York, New York 10010 [mackids.com]

Henry Holt® is a registered trademark of Henry Holt and Company, LLC.

Library of Congress Cataloging-in-Publication Data
Walker, Sally M., author.
Winnie : the true story of the bear who inspired Winnie-the-Pooh / Sally M. Walker ; illustrated by Jonathan D. Voss.
page   cm
Summary: "When Harry Colebourn saw a baby bear at a train station, he knew he could care for it. Harry was a veterinarian. But he was also a soldier in training during World War I. Harry named the bear Winnie, short for Winnipeg, his company's home town, and he brought her along to the military camp in England. Winnie followed Harry everywhere and slept under his cot every night. Before long, she became the regiment's much-loved mascot. But who could care for the bear when Harry went to battle? Harry found just the right place for Winnie—the London Zoo. There a boy named Christopher Robin played with Winnie—he could care for this bear too!"—Provided by publisher
Audience: Ages 4–8.   Includes bibliographical references.
ISBN 978-0-8050-9715-3 (hardcover)
1. Colebourn, Harry, 1887–1947—Juvenile literature. 2. Canada. Canadian Armed Forces—Mascots—Juvenile literature. 3. Winnipeg (Bear)—Juvenile literature. 4. Winnie-the-Pooh (Fictitious character)—History—Juvenile literature. 5. Black bear—Juvenile literature. I. Voss, Jonathan D., illustrator. II. Title.
QL737.C27W348 2015   599.78'5—dc23   2014028434

Henry Holt books may be purchased for business or promotional use. For information on bulk purchases, please contact Macmillan Corporate and Premium Sales Department at (800) 221-7945 x5442 or by e-mail at specialmarkets@macmillan.com.

First Edition—2015 / Designed by Véronique Lefèvre Sweet
The artist used watercolor with pen and ink on Arches Hot Press Watercolor Board
to create the illustrations for this book.
Printed in the United States of America by Phoenix Color, Hagerstown, Maryland

3 5 7 9 10 8 6 4 2

WINNIE

The True Story of the Bear
Who Inspired Winnie-the-Pooh

SALLY M. WALKER

Illustrated by JONATHAN D. VOSS

Henry Holt and Company ❦ New York

When Harry Colebourn looked out of the train window, he couldn't believe what he saw: a bear at the station! The train's stop would be short, but Harry had to get off and see the bear for himself.

Harry hurried onto the platform and sat nearby. "What are you doing here, little bear?" The cub climbed into Harry's lap and licked his chin.

"She's for sale," said the man holding her leash. "I didn't see her until after I'd shot her mother. I don't want her. *I* can't care for a bear."

Harry could care for a bear; he was a veterinarian.
"How much?" Harry asked.

"Twenty dollars."

The train whistle blew, and Harry decided. He paid the
man, picked up the cub, and carried her onto the train.

Harry's friends asked a million questions.
But the captain asked the loudest. "Harry,
what in the *world* were you thinking?"
"That I had to save her."

The cub rubbed her back against the captain's legs. The captain patted her head.

"I'll care for her, sir," Harry said. "I'll feed her condensed milk. She can stay with me in camp. Winnipeg can be our mascot."

"You've already named her?" asked the captain.

"Yes, sir! After our company's hometown."

"Well, Winnipeg," the captain said, "welcome to the army."

By the time they reached the military training camp at Valcartier, in Quebec, *Winnipeg* had been shortened to *Winnie.*

Harry's job was caring for horses that would be needed
for battle. Winnie's job was being Harry's shadow.

While Harry listened to a horse's heart, Winnie nuzzled its muzzle. If the horse snorted and scared Winnie, Harry cuddled her until she stopped trembling.

Winnie's favorite game
was hide-and-seek-biscuits.

Using her long claws,
she pulled hidden biscuits
from Harry's pockets.

"Good girl!" Harry
praised when she
succeeded.

Sometimes Harry went places where Winnie couldn't.
Then other soldiers cub-sat. They photographed Winnie.
They took her for walks.

But no matter where Winnie went during the day,
she slept under Harry's cot every night.

One morning, while Harry tied his bootlaces, Winnie
grabbed the tent pole. The tent walls shook. "Winnie,
no!" Harry shouted. After that, Harry let Winnie
climb small trees. But he always held her leash so she
couldn't climb too high.

A month passed. Then the captain received bad news. "The war across the Atlantic Ocean is getting worse. More soldiers and horses are needed. We must leave Canada and go to England. The ships will be leaving in a few days."

Harry couldn't leave Winnie! "Sir, she must come with us." The other soldiers agreed. When the horses and soldiers boarded the S.S. *Manitou*, so did Winnie.

Winnie was a good sailor. Harry wasn't.
He lay seasick in the ship's hospital.
While he was sick, Winnie played with
the other soldiers, but she ran straight
to Harry as soon as he was better.

In England, Harry, Winnie, and the horses traveled to a new military camp. For seven weeks, Winnie watched soldiers practice marching. She heard gunshots when they practiced shooting. Still, every night she slept under Harry's cot.

One day the captain said, "The war is even worse. We must go to France and care for horses that get wounded."

On a battlefield, Winnie could be hurt, even killed. Harry didn't want to leave Winnie, but he couldn't take her to France. He thought long and hard. Finally, Harry contacted the London Zoo.

"Winnie, the zoo has a brand-new place called the Mappin Terraces, which is built just for bears. Zookeepers know *exactly* how to care for a bear."

The ride to the zoo was long. Winnie sat on Harry's lap.
She wiggled on the seat. She scratched at the door. Harry
was relieved when he and Winnie got out at the zoo.

A zookeeper escorted Harry and Winnie to the Mappin
Terraces.

Harry removed Winnie's collar and leash. She climbed over a rock. She sniffed two brown cubs. She lapped condensed milk when the zookeeper offered it. Harry was satisfied. "Winnie, I'll visit whenever I can. When the war ends, we'll go home to Winnipeg." Harry hugged Winnie good-bye.

Winnie and the brown cubs became fast friends. But the big Himalayan bear she approached wasn't so friendly.

He swatted at Winnie. Winnie ran as far as she could. The zookeepers were worried. But even the grumpy Himalayan bear couldn't resist Winnie. Within a few days, they were playing tug-of-war with a stick.

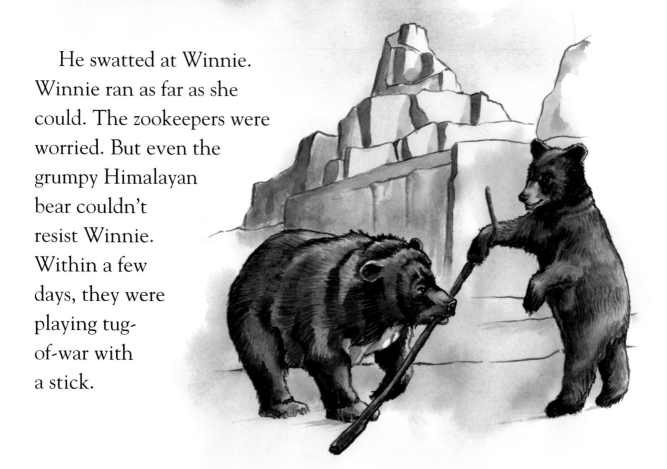

"We've never met a bear as gentle as Winnie,"
the zookeepers said. They trusted her so much that
they sometimes let children ride on her back.

Harry visited Winnie whenever he could, but the war lasted four years. During that time, the zookeepers took good care of his bear. Winnie had many friends.

In 1919, just before Harry returned to Winnipeg, he made another hard decision. He decided that Winnie would stay at the London Zoo permanently. Harry was sad, but he knew Winnie would be happiest in the home she knew best.

One day, when Winnie was nearly eleven years old, a little boy visited her. "Oh, Bear!" cried the boy, whose name was Christopher Robin. He hugged Winnie and fed her milk.

The boy's father, a well-known author, watched his son laugh and play with the bear. All the way home, Christopher Robin talked about Winnie.

At bedtime, Christopher Robin and his teddy
snuggled under the covers.

"Would you and Edward Bear like to hear a story?"
asked the boy's father.

"Yes," said Christopher Robin, "but Edward has
changed his name to Winnie-the-Pooh."

"Once upon a time," said his father, "a bear named
Winnie-the-Pooh lived in a forest." More stories
followed, until, one day, they grew into a book.

After that, the *real* Winnie became even more famous. Although more people came to see her, Winnie's everyday life remained normal. The zookeepers treated her kindly, friendly visitors scratched her back, and gentle children spoon-fed her milk. For Winnie, *this* was the best way to care for a bear.

AUTHOR'S NOTE

HARRY COLEBOURN was born April 12, 1887, in Birmingham, England. He moved to Canada as a young man. In 1911, he graduated from the Ontario Veterinary College as a veterinary surgeon. He settled in Winnipeg, Manitoba, where he worked as a veterinarian for Canada's Department of Agriculture.

Before World War I, Harry belonged to a regiment in Winnipeg called the Thirty-fourth Fort Garry Horse. On September 25, 1914, he was commissioned as a lieutenant in the Canadian Army Veterinary Corps. Later, he was attached to the Second Canadian Infantry Brigade and eventually promoted to captain. During the war, many hundreds of horses owed their lives to Harry's excellent care. At the war's end, he returned to veterinary practice in Winnipeg. Harry died on September 24, 1947.

WINNIE was an American black bear (*Ursus americanus*). Her species is native to North American forests. In the wild, they eat berries, new plant sprouts, fruits, nuts, and grasses. They also eat bees, wasps, ants (and their larva), salmon, and occasionally young mammals. Black bears hibernate during the winter. Females give birth in late January and in early February; a litter usually includes two cubs. Adult female black bears usually weigh between 100 and 300 pounds. Standing on its hind legs, a fully grown black bear is as tall as an adult human. In the wild, black bears live about twenty years; in captivity, they have lived more than ten years longer.

When Harry bought Winnie at the White River train station in Ontario, Canada, she was six to seven months old. Winnie died on May 12, 1934, at the age of twenty. News of her death and her connection to *Winnie-the-Pooh* were reported in newspapers in England, Canada, and the United States.

Winnie-the-Pooh, by A. A. Milne, was published in 1926; a sequel, *The House at Pooh Corner*, came out in 1928. Milne also wrote two books of poetry in which Winnie-the-Pooh appears: *When We Were Very Young* (1924) and *Now We Are Six* (1927). According to Milne, Christopher Robin gave the name "Pooh" to a swan he once knew. When the swan flew off and made its home elsewhere, the name remained behind, unused. Therefore, it was available to combine with "Winnie" when Christopher Robin needed it.

A statue of Harry and Winnie reminds visitors to the London Zoo of one of its most famous residents. [*Sally M. Walker*]

SOURCES

Harry D. Colebourn Fonds [Collection]. Winnipeg: Archives of Manitoba. Diary kept by Harry Colebourn during his service in the Canadian Army Veterinary Corps.

London Zoo Daily Record Books for 1914 and 1934. The Library of the London Zoo.

Shushkewich, Val. *The Real Winnie: A One-of-a-Kind Bear*. Toronto: Natural Heritage Books, 2003.

Thwaite, Ann. *The Brilliant Career of Winnie-the-Pooh: The Definitive History of the Best Bear in All the World*. New York: Dutton Children's Books, 1994.

Winnie file at the London Zoo.

WEBSITE AND VINTAGE VIDEO

www.fortgarryhorse.ca The website of the Fort Garry Horse Regiment describes the unit's service record and Harry Colebourn's history with Winnie.

www.britishpathe.com/video/secrets-of-nature-hold-all The 1930 *Secrets of Nature* video "Hold All" shows animals at the London Zoo. Winnie makes a brief appearance about two minutes and forty-five seconds into the nine-minute-long review. Pro Patria film.

Winnie eagerly licked the spoon when zookeepers fed her condensed milk. [*Zoological Society of London*]

Author A. A. Milne and his son, Christopher Robin, pose with Edward Bear. Christopher Robin renamed his teddy Winnie-the-Pooh. [*National Portrait Gallery, London*]